Under the Sun

Under the Sun

a chapbook of poems

by Kevin Hulit

By the Bay Media

Under the Sun

Copyright © 2018 By the Bay Media LLC

ISBN: 978-1-7321168-4-9

First Printing in 2018

www.bythebaymedia.com

For
Mom

Contents

Wolves

Through emerald forests
hunted dreamers run,
roaming the wild
over countless nights,
howling for the sun.

Sharp-fanged rovers
howl a wild song,
a sad story
of burdened beasts,
their search for salvation
under a dark moon's madness,
in a land that was once
their own.

A Morning After Snow

The cold dawn glistens
on crests of crusted snow.
Frigid breath lingers,
forming a cloud -
faint and frozen.

The meadow is buried,
a blizzard's work completed.
Barren branches lay severed
below a lonely oak
centered in the meadow.
Twigs breach the snow,
skeletal fingers
reaching for the rising sun,
remembering its warmth.

The quietness that comes
with midnight snow
vanishes at first light.
Birds stir,
singing songs of wild strengths,
triumphant
over the harsh winter night.

Pristine snow
veils the field from edge to edge,
as well as the trees lining the meadow,
fat in their new white coats.
The beauty is fleeting,
lasting only as long
as the gentle sunrise,
or until the memory of it fades.

Winter Song

Ice-covered trees
sing harmonies
of creaks and moans,
and low earthy tones,
as the blizzard winds batters them.
Bark and branch sway,
passing chills through limbs.
A winter song.
A woodwind composition playing on,
while wintry gray giants
bend in the cold.
Memories of summer
warm their heartwood,
as the runnel trickles a sonata
below them.

Trees of Glass

Trees of glass
gleam in the sun,
a golden casing glimmering
on frozen twigs and limbs,
an ice world shining
despite the harsh night
that bore it.

Winter Solstice

Oh, darkness.
Oh, longest night.
I suffer you today
knowing tomorrow
you will lose
to the light -
a tiny flesh wound,
followed by
death
from a slow bleed.

A Heavy Stone

The memories
of this heavy stone,
a child's feet
padding along
a north woods boulder,
nearly a planet of its own
by the gauge of young eyes.
An adventurer
upon this glacial gift,
given eons ago.

The highwaters of spring,
rushing along,
are moved aside
by the monumental rock.
Whitecaps and swirls
dance away downstream,
upon bouncing off
its hardened façade.

Forest mosses,
splashed in the interplay,
hold firmly to the giant,
always here,
year upon year.
A heavy stone.
A memory.

Song for the Sea

Amid the rain,
when into the fog
the horizon has retreated,
when the ocean seems empty,
angry and loud -
the mists in the wind
combine me
with the salt of the sea.

From high on dunes
I sing to the water,
wonderous and supreme.
Foamy waves
roar against the shore,
as if
to join me.
There is majesty in the harmony.
I sing to the waves
that crash and press on,
that sing with me today,
and will sing when I am gone.

Sky

Boundless blue,
endless view,
ever to know
all there is;
the sun,
the rain,
the clouds.
The stars that show,
and the storms that blow,
all pieces
of an omnipresent sky,
reigning above
the land and sea,
and a billion eyes gazing.
The aurora of night,
the full moon's light,
hover high above a world,
amazed.

Rebirth

Delicate limbs hang from a willow,
ragged and old.
They sway in the gentle winds they catch,
then let go.
Draped tiredly
in a cold-water stream,
they bathe their young leaves
among near silent stones,
and the highwaters of spring.

Perched upon the bark,
huddled in the cover,
hidden from the rain,
a momentary rest
from long and travelled days -
a returning warbler
renews itself,
humbled
by its journey home.

In the air there is rebirth.
The continuance of life.
The wind and rain
ramble on,
a sweet conversation
of sweet little nothings,
as days grow longer
with delicate moments.

Twilight's Murmur

A sliver moon
beams low on the horizon,
a glow of gold
nested softly in the sky,
hovering silently
just above the tree line.
Day kisses night
in a smear of pink blushes,
Mother Nature's paint
on a canvas of endless heaven.
The pinks and purples
of twilight's murmur,
a softly spoken goodnight,
after a sweet but rushed hello.

Mud of Spring

I pray for the mud of spring,
for seeds from the harvest
to return to the earth,
for a life sated
by the laboring for fruit,
for the sun-dried dirt
on my cracked worn hands,
ready to be taken by the wind,
to be bound to the rain,
to begin a spring again.

Soft Hellos

The downfall of winter comes
upon spring's subtle rise,
the cold subjugation ending
with the arrival of gentle petals
from blooming buds.

Winds blow softly,
resembling warm sighs -
an intimate touch
to melt away the cold
with a sun's worth
of soft hellos.

The River

In the river
runs life's splendors.
The scent of water
warmed by touches
from the springtime sun,
fills hearts with promises
yet to come.

In the river,
Sounds play
a subtle song -
the constant rush of riffles,
the dull knocking of stones
muted by the water,
songs heard best
when heard alone.

In the river
water covers stone,
rounding rough edges
along the riverbed.
These stones I hold,
and know that I am home.

In my hands
water from the river
fails to stand,
falling from my reach,
or what I can feel -
in the river
the water holds me.

A day in the river
with nowhere else to be,
the peace and serenity
purify me.

Harbinger

Little bird,
harbinger of spring,
a softly sung melody
gliding in
on worn feathers
and wayward wings.
Sing in trees,
feathered friend,
amid the budding blooms
freed from the frost.
The cold has gone.
The sun
has come.
Rejoice in the warmth
these longer days bring.

Water Weeds

Water weeds
struggle
where the river
meets the air,
pulled
by currents
forever flowing.
Some break free
and float away,
others
never let go.

Clouds

Free within
a boundless sky,
no destination,
or defined expectation,
forever changing,
shaping shapelessly.
Bright giants
gliding in the sky,
the gentle dance
of the carefree,
tangible,
yet always beyond -
elegance,
opposed only
by the storm
that builds
within.

The Equality of Rain

The drilling of drops
on the ground,
on my skin,
a holy cleansing
washing away the grime.
A cleaned slate.
Then back to the beginning
to muck it up again.
Rain.
Sate the thirst of the land,
and of man.
Fuel growth
in deep-rooted souls
leaning toward the sun
in row upon row,
depositing a sustenance
seeded for others.
On the crop of human courses,
the drench covers all
in sheets of equal rainfall.
Among the many,
my soul,
worshiping the soggy spirits
of this wetted world.
A gush of solace,
splashed up from puddles,
spreads across the sodden earth,
my boots sloshing a hymnal,
kicking up mud
on all my worth,
the raindrops falling,
tiny beads of solitude,
uniting my footsteps
with the world.

To the North

To the north,
my friend,
to summers
of white-throated sparrows,
rock walls
along wildflower meadows,
lake swimming,
and walks
in boreal forests.

Sunset on a Mountainside

A silent warmth
covers the mountainside.
Soft pinks
and orange glows
smother the hard rock
of the alpine.
The onset of night idles
in the quietude
of a wild sunset.

A Tree in a Storm

I saw the way
the treetop
bent,

the weight
of the storm
too great
to withstand,

the grip
of its needles
too strong
to let go.

The fall
in the end,
meant to be,
I suppose.

Time to Be

On the forest floor,
among spent leaves
and other wind-worn things,
footfalls from woodland beings
gently crush fallen twigs
in the pervasive quiet.
No sounds beyond
a chirping sparrow
hidden in the trees,
and the subdued squeaks
of a chickadee
looking up
at this world as well
so far-reaching,
ever grasping at the light,
so removed from life on the ground -
here where there is no sound.
The solitude of trees,
of standing amid slender giants,
their arms outreached
to steal the sun,
create a temple,
strong and pious.
The green that grows
covers all below,
holding still
the world within.
In every direction
tree and life are tethered,
so thick and dense,
dissolving direction altogether.
There is only
the woods,
the trees,
and time
to be.

The Lake

Hummingbirds and honeybees
set to work among summer's colors,
as a midday concerto
of sylvan woodwind,
avian brass,
and entomic strings,
performs in its natural cadence.
Leaves applaud,
as the loyal and tender wind
nurtures their fandom,
carrying it
from one shore
to the other.
Ripples disrupt the stillness
of a morning's work,
sending out accolades
as sun glares and whitecaps
on the water.
Moments of sunshine
ramble through
a canopy of green,
so that that blue of day
can view the song
from its high seat.
The warmth it brings
embraces,
before it is carried away
in the subtle breeze.
White birch trees and identical ferns
devotedly sway
in reverence to the performance.
I may be but a visitor,
wandered into a song,
but amid these notes,
these sounds of summer,
I am forever home.

New England Meadow

Hidden by woods,
a meadow
in the middle of a town.
Wildflower blooms
fill the field,
as tree swallows swoop
amid sweet sounding songs.
Warm breezes
rule the air
under the summer sun.
The smell of tall grasses
travel along
the rock wall -
a childhood memory,
a heart's home.

Sounds of Summer

Sit in a simmer
of the sounds of summer.
Bird songs serenade
the early morning sun -
a farewell to the night,
so that day may come.

A summer's midday
holds sound quietly.
The fauna,
if moving,
moves faintly and smartly.

A symphony
of summer bugs
fills the evening air.
Orchestral sounds
pierce the darkness
everywhere.

Oh, summer days,
the sun's gift to all,
a crescendo of the living
before the diminuendo
of the fall.

Dragonfly

The sun!
The sun!
Summer has come!
Steam-stuffed air,
hazing the sky,
is cut
by the wings
of a dragonfly.
Through the garden
its four wings hum,
aeronautical star,
hunter on the wing,
carnivore of summer,
in full splendor,
thriving.
A whir of color and speed
rip through the air,
humid days,
and sun-kissed nights,
when dragonflies
live to take flight.

Leaves

Drained yellow leaves
flutter in the sway,
their weakening holds
on a tired tree,
now turning them away.
To the wind they rush,
or to the ground they fall,
the end of a season,
for one and all.

Fire

A single star
faintly presides
over a smoky veil
from a fleeting fire.
The last embers
fade away,
gone
like the others
that burned
before them,
along with
the wilderness
that bore them.

To Feel a Breeze

I am adrift.
I have quit the race -
happy to run
at a human pace.
To smell a rose,
to feel a breeze,
to hear the hum
of pollinating bees.
To watch the sun
tragically set,
only to see it
rise again.

A Pond with Punks and Ducks

In a field
on a farm,
just beyond
the side yard,
over the rock wall,
downhill from the barn -
there rests the little pond.

Around the dock
swim two mallard ducks.
Around the pond
grow tall punks.
They hide the ducks
from this little boy's view,
their feathers unseen
but heard is their mew.

From the shoulders of my father,
I could see the ducks,
the water,
and a little bit farther.
I loved that pond
we often walked by,
and the ducks,
and the punks,
and those days
now gone.

Night and Day

Subtle winds
stir softly
through the leaves.
The night brings silence,
steady in the faint light
from a crescent moon
and clement stars,
true companions
in a forever of nights.
A backdrop of endlessness
behind their slow dance,
their peaceful glow
shining bright,
repeatedly devoured
by the violent daylight.

Kevin Hulit

Wilderness

Lupines grow
where mountains can see,
where rivers flow
and salmon swim free.
Bears and wolves,
wild bees.

A wilderness of green,
trees unseen,
untouched waters.
Harmony.

Brook Trout

Colors veiled
by a shield of water,
natural beauty
living in riffles,
a simple life
of swim,
and eat,
swim,
and repeat.
Clean
cold
water,
such humble pleasures,
vital
to this
cherished fish.

Dirt

All that dies,
dies for the dirt,
from which
arises,
life on earth.

Dirt is life.
Life is dirt,
and within each
are those
who've lived,
and loved,
and lost.

With no judgements,
dirt gives and takes,
collecting bones
and stories,
silently.

October Night

So cool the air
on gentle winds come,
from earlier evenings
and a weakening sun.

Through open windows,
so cool the air seeps.
Heavy blankets
warm the flesh,
as tired bodies sleep.

Through open windows,
the rustle of leaves,
some dead,
some living,
all meant to meet
their last day
on the ground,
scattered,
or swept away,
to where the wind ends.

Beautiful night,
dark,
and smoky,
fires in homes nearby
send smoke through chimneys,
to join the air,
so cool,
so right.
Heaven is
an October night.

Kevin Hulit

Sunday Morning

Sunday morning,
the chill of autumn reaches
through open windows,
as geese fly south
in a low formation,
waking us
in our little house in Harvard,
where we ate from the garden,
walked in the woods,
and laughed on walks along rock walls,
passing the horses and the fields
on our way to the orchard,
for a few apples to steal.

Autumn Life

Leaves,
nearly yellow,
shine in the afternoon sun,
a collection of shadows,
silhouettes of branch and bark,
mix with the brilliance
of their golden glow.
Crickets chirp of loneliness
in the cooling air,
the chill in the woods
compliments the solitude
that calls man away
into nature.
Autumn life.
The passing of summer
brings beauty to full bloom,
long after the blossoms
have all gone.
This momentary time
fosters a oneness with the forest
that evades the other seasons,
the full recognition
of the natural splendor,
a final burst
of everything's best
before it all ends,
falling to the ground
to be buried in the snow,
as cold memories of color.

Wind in Reeds

A feeling,
serene,
in the fading sun's gleam,
Soft edges
on dried reeds
tickle the wind
lingering through,
a blow-in bending
with no intention.

The Last of Crickets

The last of crickets
solos an elegy
for summer,
recalling lost symphonies
in slow measures
of a fading song,
final notes
to haunt the cold.

Made in the USA
Lexington, KY
19 March 2019